BIBLE
STUDY SERIES

BIBLE
STUDY SERIES
1 Samuel - Part 1

PASTOR RAMONA BROWN

 www.trafford.com
North America & international
toll-free: 1 888 232 4444 (USA & Canada)
fax: 812 355 4082

CONTENTS

BACKGROUND

History

The 1st and 2nd books of Samuel, found in the Old Testament, were written by Samuel, David, Nathan, and Gad between 1204-1035 B.C. in Palestine, and was finally made one book by Isaiah the prophet circa 743-683 (see 1 Chronicles 29:29). The books of Samuel were originally one book in the Hebrew Canon. The single volume of Samuel was divided into two volumes by the translators of the Greek Old Testament (the Septuagint) who viewed the books of Samuel and Kings together as the "Books of the Kingdom." The book of Kings was likewise divided into two books.

The books of Samuel contain more than biographical and historical interest. The central theme of the books trace God's gracious and overruling sovereignty in the sad state of affairs in Israel at the end of the period of judges by His providential selection of righteous men (i.e., Samuel and David) who would weld the nation into an instrument of His will and a people for Himself. Despite Israel's rejection of God as King, God would prove faithful and eventually see to the appointment of a godly king, David, with whom He would enter into an everlasting covenant that would affect the destiny of both Israel and the entire world, for through David would come Israel's King, Messiah and the Savior of the world, the Lord Jesus Christ.

Facts about the Book of Samuel

- 9th book of the Bible
- 31 chapters

- 810 verses
- 25,061 words
- 167 questions
- 50 verses of fulfilled prophecy
- 1 verse of unfulfilled prophecy
- 29 distinct messages from God
- 4 promises
- 117 commands
- 57 predictions
- Recounts the last days of the judges
- Chronicles the moral failure of the priesthood under Eli
- Illustrates the moral failure of the judges under Samuel
- Chronicles the beginning and failure of the monarchy under Saul
- Introduces David as a warrior and a possible successor to the throne.

WHO'S WHO

1. **SAMUEL**—*Asked of God*

   - Prophet and overseer of Israel

2. **ELKANAH**—*God has possessed*

   - Father of Samuel
   - Grandson of Korah (Exodus 6:24)
   - Husband of Peninnah and Hannah

3. **HANNAH**—*Grace and favor*

   - Mother of Samuel
   - Wife of Elkanah

4. **PENINNAH**—*Pear*

   - Wife of Elkanah
   - Provoked Hannah

5. **ELI**—*God is high*

   - 15th Judge of Israel—Shiloh.
   - Reigned for 40 years
   - 7th high priest of Israel

6. **HOPHNI**—*Pugilist*

   - Son of Eli

- Served as priest
- Considered a wicked priest because he engaged in illicit behavior

7. **PHINEHAS**—*Mouth of brass or serpent's mouth*

- Second son of Eli
- Disgraced his priestly role because of irreverent and immoral behavior

8. **KING SAUL**—*Asked For*

- Son of Kish
- Anointed by Samuel to be the first king of Israel

9. **JONATHAN**—*God given*

- First born son of King Saul
- Led 1,000 men in defeating the Philistines at Gibeah (1 Samuel 13:2-3)

10. **DAVID**—*Beloved*

- Shepherd Boy
- Slayed the giant, Goliath
- King of Israel

11. **ABIGAIL**—*A father's joy*

- Wife of King David

FULFILLED PROPHECY
IN SAMUEL 1

1. **1 Samuel 2:1-10**

   - This fulfilled the prophecy that the Messiah would be called a Nazarene.
   - (See Psalm 22 . . . and is taken largely from the song of Hannah)

2. **1 Samuel 2:27 and 1 Samuel 4:1-22**

   - Prophecy of judgment against Eli.
   - The Ark was taken from the house of Eli.

3. **1 Samuel 3:11-14**

   - Prophecy of judgment against Eli's sons.
   - (See 1 Samuel 4:1-22 and 1 Kings 2:26-27)

4. **1 Samuel 9:16-20**

   - God instructs Samuel to anoint Saul as leader of His people.

5. **1 Samuel 10:1-13**

   - This fulfilled the prophecy that Saul would prophesy among the prophets.

6. **1 Samuel 12:1-25 and 1 Samuel 31:1-13**

- Samuel warns the people of Israel about their wickedness towards God.
- King Saul and his sons die at the hands of the Philistines.

7. **1 Samuel 16:1-23; 2 Samuel 2:1-11 and 2 Samuel 5:1-12**

- Saul is rejected as King of Israel.
- David is anointed King of Judah after the death of King Saul.
- David is anointed King of Israel after the death of King Saul.

PLAGUES AND MIRACULOUS EVENTS

In 1 Samuel 5 we see that the Philistines did not know that taking the ark, which was Israel's symbol of the glory of God, would cause divine judgment to fall on them. When they took the sacred and consecrated things, and dedicated to their own gods and then gloated over the powerlessness of God, they caused God's divine judgment to fall.

Ashdod was one of the five chief cities of the Philistines. This name means stronghold or fortress, the seat of worship for the god Dagon. Dagon was the national God of the Philistines and was shaped like part man and fish. His temples were at Gaza and Ashdod.

God begins to perform the following miracles of judgments upon the Philistines:

- The overthrow of Dagon—an angel toppled Dagon from his pedestal on his face before the ark of the Lord as if in homage to the God of Israel (v2-3).
- The destruction of Dagon—his face was before the ark with his head and hands cut off (v 4-5).
- The supernatural plague of emerods in all of Ashdod and surrounding country (v 6).
- The supernatural plague upon Gath, of emerods in the secret parts (5:7-9)
- The supernatural plague of deadly destruction upon the people of Ekron (v 10-11).

- The plague of emerods upon the people of Ekron who did not die in the plague of death (v 12).
- The 2 cows who took the cart back to Israel (6 v 7-12)
- The supernatural destruction of men of Beth-shemesh (6:19)

In the Hebrew, the word "tumor" means ophel from aphal and it means to swell. Emerods is an old spelling of the modern hemorrhoids (bleeding piles). The hand of the Lord expresses the power of God. His power was manifested in a miraculous way upon them—the sudden appearance of this plague is what made this clear to have been supernatural.

It took the Philistines seven months to learn their lesson that taking the ark from place to place did not solve their problem, but spread the plague to other places. They wanted to keep the ark if possible. For it was a prize to dedicate to their national god Dagon. The offering of trespass they sent was five golden mice and emerods, which represented the five lords of the Philistines.

The emerods marred their bodies and the mice marred their land. In this story we see three (3) objects of God's judgment:

1. You (philistines) (v 5:5, 6, 9, 11-12)
2. Your gods (philistines) (5:1-3, 7)
3. Your land (philistines) (v 5)

How do we recognize God's judgments and plagues in this day and time?

A plague is described as any sudden or severe disease. It can also be mysterious and an affliction sent by God as punishment for sin and disobedience. In most cases in the Bible, the affliction is an epidemic or disease. The Greek word for plague literally means a blow or a lash, implying punishment or chastisement.

Plagues appear throughout the biblical record. The first mention of a plague in Scripture was that sent on Pharaoh for the protection of Sarah, Abraham's wife (Gen 12:17). The next plagues were the ten afflictions experienced by the Egyptians when the Pharaoh refused to release the Hebrew people from bondage. While these plagues were phenomena with which the Egyptians were familiar, they exhibited miraculous features that were characteristic of God's judgment. Later, during the years of the Exodus, a plague was sent upon the Hebrews for making and worshiping a golden calf (Ex 32:35). Another occurred because of their murmuring against the food which God provided for them (Num 11:33-34). The spies who brought faithless reports about the Promised Land were inflicted with a plague (Num 14:37).

The plagues were sometimes miraculous events. At other times they appeared as natural phenomena. But they always represented God's aggressive acts to punish sin and disobedience among His people.

POLYGAMY

Polygamy was tolerated under the law (*Exodus 21:10; Deuteronomy 21:15-17*) and before the gospel program (*Acts 17:30*), but it was forbidden in the New Testament (*Matthew 19:4-5; Mark 10:1-8; 1 Timothy 3:2 and 12; Titus 1:6*). We see that Samuel was born to a woman whose husband had two wives.

There are 15 accounts of polygamy in the Old Testament:

1. Lamech (Genesis 4:19-23)
2. Abraham (Genesis 16 and 25)
3. Esau (Genesis 26:34; 28:9)
4. Jacob (Genesis 29:16; 30:24)
5. Gideon (Judges 8:30)
6. David (1 Samuel 25:39-44; 2 Samuel 3:2-5; 5:13; 1 Chronicles 14:3)
7. Solomon (Kings 11:1-8)
8. Rehoboam (2 Chronicles 11:18-23)
9. Ashur (1 Chronicles 4:5)
10. Abijah (2 Chronicles 13:21)
11. Jehoram (2 Chronicles 21:14)
12. Joash (2 Chronicles 21:14)
13. Ahab (2 Kings 10:1)
14. Jehoiachin (2 Kings 24:15)
15. Belshazzar (Daniel 5:2)

PROPHET, PRIEST, AND JUDGE

Chapter 1

Samuel's life was the result of effectual, fervent prayer by a praying, loving mother, a mother who loved the Lord with all of her heart. Hannah's heart cry for a son, which was aggravated by Penninah's insolence, but in some measure balanced by her husband's kindness; the prayer and vow she made to God under this affliction, in which Eli the high priest at first censured her but afterwards encouraged her; the birth and nursing of Samuel; and the presenting of him to the Lord is the focal point of this chapter. (*Matthew Henry's Commentary on the Whole Bible, p. 380*)

Chapter 2

Chapter 2 illustrates Hannah's thanksgiving to God for his favor in giving her a son; their return to their family, with Eli's blessing; the increase of their family; Samuel's growth and improvement and the care Hannah took to clothe him; the great wickedness of Eli's sons; the over-mild reproof that Eli gave them for it; and the justly dreadful message God sent him by a prophet, threatening the ruin of his family for the wickedness of his sons. (*Matthew Henry's Commentary on the Whole Bible, p. 383*)

Chapter 3

In this chapter, we see Samuel as the young prophet, which was more God in an extraordinary manner revealing Himself to Samuel and in him reviving, if not commencing prophecy in Israel. Here is God's first manifestation of Himself in an extraordinary manner to Samuel; the message he sent by him to Eli; the faithful delivery of that message to Eli, and his submission to the righteousness of God in it; and the establishment of Samuel to be a prophet in Israel. (*Matthew Henry's Commentary on the Whole Bible, p. 386*)

Scripture Search: Exercise 1

Find the Following Scriptures:

1. "Why weepest thou? And thou eatest not? And why is thy heart grieved? Am I not better to thee than ten sons?" **1 Samuel 1:_____**

2. "How long will thou be drunken?" **1 Samuel 1:_____**

3. "Why do ye such things?" **1 Samuel 1:_____**

4. "But if a man sin against the Lord, who shall entreat for him?" **1 Samuel 1:_____**

5. "Did I plainly appear unto the house of thy father, when they were in Egypt in Pharaoh's house?" **1 Samuel 2:_____**

6. "To offer upon mine altar, to burn incense, to wear an ephod before me?" **1 Samuel 2:_____**

7. "I give unto the house of they father all the offerings made by fire of the children of Israel?" **1 Samuel 2:_____**

8. "And the LORD said to Samuel: "See, I am about to do something in Israel that will make the ears of everyone who hears of it tingle." **1 Samuel 3:_____**

9. "And he said, what is the thing that the Lord hath said unto thee?"
1 Samuel 3:_____

10. "The LORD continued to appear at Shiloh, and there he revealed himself to Samuel through his word." **1 Samuel 3:**_____

Fill in the Blank: Exercise 2

1. And he had two wives; the name of the one was Hannah, and the name of the other Peninnah. _____ had children, but _____ had no children.

2. Count not thine handmaid for a daughter of Belial: for out of the abundance of my _____ and _____ have I spoken hitherto.

3. And thou shalt see an enemy in my _____, in all the wealth which God shall give _____: and there shall not be an old man in thine house forever.

4. And all Israel from Dan even to _____ knew that Samuel was established to be a prophet of the LORD.

Circle the Correct Word: Exercise 3

1. So Hannah rose up after they had eaten in Shiloh, and after they had _____. Now Eli the priest sat upon a seat by a post of the temple of the LORD.

   DRUNK   **EATEN**

2. And the man Elkanah, and all his house, went up to offer unto the LORD the yearly _____, and his vow.

   SACRIFICE   **BLESSING**

3. And the LORD came, and stood, and _____ as at other times, Samuel, Samuel. Then Samuel _____, "Speak; for thy servant heareth."

CALLED   **SPOKEN**   **ANSWERED**   **RAN**

True or False: Exercise 4

1. The LORD called Samuel: and he answered, go away.

TRUE OR FALSE

2. Now the sons of Eli were sons of Belial; they knew not the LORD.

TRUE OR FALSE

READING ASSIGNMENT

1. The Shiloh traditions. (1 Samuel 1:1-3)

2. Samuel's birth and dedication. (1 Samuel 1:19-20)

3. Hannah dedicates Samuel. (1 Samuel 1:21-22)

4. Hannah's prayer. (1 Samuel 2:1-11)

5. Eli's sons are considered evil. (1 Samuel 2:12:16)

6. The sins of Eli's sons. (1 Samuel 2:17)

8. Hannah's annual visit to Shiloh. (1 Samuel 2:18-21)

9. Eli's rebuke of his sinful sons. (1 Samuel 2:22-26)

10. House of Eli denounced. (1 Samuel 2:27-36)

11. Yahweh's appearance to Samuel. (1 Samuel 3:1-4)

12. Samuel had the favor of the Lord from his youth. (1 Samuel 3:19-21)

REFLECTIONS

THE MOVING OF THE ARK

Chapter 4

The predictions in the foregoing chapters concerning the ruin of Eli's house begin to be fulfilled—the disgrace and loss Israel sustained in an encounter with the Philistines; their foolish project to fortify themselves by bringing the ark of God into their camp upon the shoulders of Hophni and Phinehas, which made them secure and struck a fear into the Philistines, but such a fear as roused them; the fatal consequences of it: Israel was beaten and the ark taken prisoner; the tidings of this brought to Shiloh and the sad reception of those tidings; the city was put into confusion; Eli fainted, fell and broke his neck. Upon hearing what had occurred, Eli's daughter-in-law went into labor and bore a son, but died immediately thereafter. (*Matthew Henry's Commentary on the Whole Bible*, p. *388*)

Chapter 5

It is now time to enquire what has become of the ark of God; we cannot but think that we shall hear more of that sacred treasure. Many have softness enough to lament the loss of the ark that have not hardiness enough to take one step towards the recovery of it, any more than Israel here. If the ark will help itself it may, for they will not help it. Unworthy they were of the name of Israelites that could thus tamely part with the glory of Israel. God would therefore take the work into his own hands and plead his own cause, since men would not appear for him.

This chapter outlines how the Philistines triumphed over the ark; how the ark triumphed over the Philistines, over Dagon their god, over the Philistines themselves, who were sorely plagued with emerods, and made weary of the ark; the men of Ashdod first, then the men of Gath, and lastly, those of Ekron, which forced them at length upon a resolution to send the ark back to the land of Israel; for when God judgeth he will overcome. (*Matthew Henry's Commentary on the Whole Bible, p. 390*)

Chapter 6

In this chapter, we have the return of the ark to the land of Israel and observe how the Philistines dismissed it by the advice of their priests with rich presents to the God of Israel, to make an atonement for their sin, and yet with a project to bring it back, unless Providence directed the kine, contrary to their inclination, to go to the land of Israel; and how the Israelites entertained it with great joy and sacrifices of praise, with an over-bold curiosity to look into it, for which many of them were struck dead, the terror of which moved them to send it forward to another city. (*Matthew Henry's Commentary on the Whole Bible, p. 391*)

IMPORTANT TERMS

1. **Shiloh** means *Peacemaker*

2. **Ashdod** means *fortress or stronghold*

3. **Ashdod to Gath** means *winepress*

4. **Gath to Ekron** means *barren place*

5. **Ekron to Beth-shemesh** means *house of the son*

6. **Beth-shemesh to Kirjath-jearim** means *city of forests*

Scripture Search: Exercise 5

Find the Following Scriptures:

1. "Wherefore hath the Lord smitten us to day before the Philistines?"
   1 Samuel 4:_____

2. "What meanest the noise of this great shout in the camp of the Hebrews?"
   1 Samuel 4:_____

3. "Who shall deliver us out of the hand of these mighty Gods?"
   1 Samuel 4:_____

4. "What meanest the noise of this tumult?" **1 Samuel 4:**_____

5. "What is there done my son?" **1 Samuel 4:**_____

6. "What shall we do with the ark of the god of Israel?"
   1 Samuel 5:_____

7. "What shall we do to the ark of the Lord?" **1 Samuel 6:**_____

8. "What shall be the trespass offering which we shall return to him?"
   1 Samuel 6:_____

9. "Wherefore then do ye harden your hearts, as the Egyptians and Pharaoh hardened their hearts?" **1 Samuel 6:**_____

10. "Who is able to stand before this holy Lord God?"
    1 Samuel 6:_____

Fill in the Blank: Exercise 6

1. Be strong and quit yourselves like men, O ye Philistines, that ye be not servants unto the _____, as they have been to you: quit yourselves like men, and fight.

2. And she named the child Ichabod, saying, The glory is _____ from Israel: because the ark of God was taken, and because of her father in law and her _____.

3. But the hand of the LORD was heavy upon them of Ashdod, and he _____ them, and smote them with emerods, even Ashdod and the coasts thereof.

4. And they laid the ark of the LORD upon the cart, and the coffer with the _____ of gold and the images of their emerods.

Circle the Correct Word: Exercise 7

1. Be strong and quit yourselves like men, O ye _____, that ye be not servants unto the Hebrews, as they have been to you: quit yourselves like men, and fight.

   PHILISTINES   **ISRAEL**

2. Therefore neither the priests of Dagon, nor any that come into Dagon's house, tread on the threshold of Dagon in _____ unto this day.

   ASHOD   **HAGGAI**

3. And the men did so; and took two milch kine, and tied them to the cart, and shut up their _____ at home:

CALVES   **HORSE**

True or False: Exercise 8

1. And when the five lords of the Philistines had seen it, they returned to Ekron the same day.

TRUE OR FALSE

2. Woe unto us! who shall deliver us out of the hand of these mighty giants? These are the Gods that smote the Egyptians with all the plagues in the wilderness.

TRUE OR FALSE

READING ASSIGNMENT

1. The Philistines capture the ark. (1 Samuel 4:3-4)

2. Eli's son are killed. (1 Samuel 4:10-11)

3. The death of Eli. (1 Samuel 4:17-18)

4. The birth of Ichabod. (1 Samuel 4:19-22)

5. The ark brings terror to the Philistines. (1 Samuel 5:1-12)

6. The return of the ark. (1 Samuel 6:1-21)

REFLECTIONS

ISRAEL LOOKS FOR A KING

Chapter 7

This chapter outlines the eclipsing of the glory of the ark by its privacy in Kirjath-jearim for many years; the appearing of the glory of Samuel in his public services for the good of Israel to whom he was raised up to be a judge, and he was the last that bore that character. This chapter gives us all the account we have of him when he was in the prime of his time; for what we had before was in his childhood; what we have of him after was in his old age. We have him here active the reformation of Israel from their idolatry; in the reviving of religion among them; in praying for them against the invading Philistines over whom God, in answer to his prayer, gave them a glorious victory; in erecting a thankful memorial of that victory; in the improvement of that victory; and in the administration of justice. (*Matthew Henry's Commentary on the Whole Bible, p. 393*)

Chapter 8

Things went so very well with Israel in the chapter before, under Samuel's administration, that it is a pity to find him so quickly, as we do in this chapter, old, and going off, and things working towards a revolution. But so it is; Israel's good days seldom continue long. We see Samuel decaying; his sons degenerating; and Israel discontented with the present government and anxious to see a change. They petition Samuel to set a king over them. Samuel brings the matter to God. God directs him what answer to give them by way of reproof and by way of remonstrance, setting forth the consequences of a change of the government, and how uneasy they would soon be under it. They insist upon their petition. Samuel promises them, from God, that they shall shortly be gratified. (*Matthew Henry's Commentary on the Whole Bible, p. 395*)

Chapter 9

Samuel had promised Israel that they should have a king. It is strange that the next news is not of candidates setting up for the government, making an interest in the people, or recommending themselves to Samuel, and by him to God to be put in nomination. Why does not the prince of the tribe of Judah look about him now, remembering Jacob's entail of the sceptre on that tribe? Is there never a bold aspiring man in Israel, to say, "I will be king, if God will choose me?" No, none appears, whether it is owing to a culpable mean-spiritedness or a laudable humility; but surely it is what can scarcely be paralleled in the history of any kingdom; a crown, such a crown, set up, and nobody bids for it. Most governments began in the ambition of the prince to rule, but Israel's in the ambition of the people to be ruled. Had any of those elders who petitioned for a king afterwards petitioned to be king, I should have suspected that person's ambition to have been at the bottom of the motion; but now (let them have the praise of what was good in them) it was not so. God having in the law, undertaken to choose their king (Deut. 27:15), they all sit still, till they hear from heaven, and that they do in this chapter, which begins the story of Saul, their first king, and, by strange steps of Providence, brings him to Samuel to be anointed privately, and so to be prepared for an election by lot, and a public commendation to the people, which follows in the next chapter.

Here is a short account of Saul's parentage and person; a large and particular account of the bringing of him to Samuel, to whom he had been before altogether a stranger. God, by revelation, had told Samuel to expect him. God, by providence, led him to Samuel. Being sent to seek his father's asses, he was at a loss. By the advice of his servant, he determined to consult Samuel. By the direction of the young maidens, he found him out. Samuel, being informed of God concerning him, treated him with respect in the gate, in the dining-room, and at length in private, where he prepared him to hear the surprising news that he must be king. And these beginnings would have been very hopeful and promising if it had not been that the sin of the people was the spring of this great affair. (*Matthew Henry's Commentary on the Whole Bible, p. 397*)

Samuel gives a word to Israel with the promise of deliverance from the Philistines and gives them five (5) conditions:

- Return to God with all of my heart.
- Put away all strange gods.
- Put away Ashtaroth (female god of Sidon and other nations).
- Prepare hearts unto God.
- Serve Him only.

I. ISRAEL PREPARES FOR VICTORY

- They put away Baalim and Ashtaroth.

- They served the Lord only.

- They gathered together for prayers.

- They poured out water as a symbol of pouring out their hearts to God in prayer.

- They fasted before Jehovah.

- They confessed their sins against God.

- They received judgment by Samuel and maxde all things right with one another.

- They depended upon the prophet and God for deliverance from their enemies.

- The offered a sacrifice and prayed for their enemies.

- They cried to God while in danger.

II. FACTS

- Kirjath-jearim was about 8 miles northeast of Beth-shemesh. The ark was brought to Abinadab (father of liberality) and Eleazar, his son, was sanctified to keep it and it remained until 20 years.

- Israel was forbidden by the Philistines to have national gatherings. So when the Philistines heard about the gathering, they knew their treaty had been broken.

- Samuel was a Levite, and according to 1 Chronicles 23:27-31, he could offer sacrifices. However, according to Numbers 18:3, he could not act in the holy place. Samuel made several sacrifices to the Lord, and God heard Samuel's prayer and not the prayers of the people.

- Beth-car means "house of a lamb"—then Samuel took a stone and set it between Mizpeh and Shen and called the name of it Ebenezer saying, "hitherto hath the Lord helped us."

- "Then God gave them peace for about 40 years . . ." This means all the days of his judgeship before they asked for a king, not all the days of his life.

- There were judges during the 450 years of Israel's history after the division of Canaan, to the time of Samuel (Acts 13:20).

Samuel becomes a circuit judge. His house was at Ramah, the four courts in his circuit (7:16-17)

- Bethel in Ephraim, approximately 12 miles north of Jerusalem.

- Gilgal in Judah, approximately 18 to 20 miles east of Jerusalem.

- Mizpeh in Benjamin, approximately 8 miles north of Jerusalem; Mizpeh in Gilead, approximately 40 miles from Jerusalem, on the east of Jordan.

- Ramah, the place where Samuel lived and would ultimately return.

- Samuel was about 20 years old when Eli died.

- Samuel served 40 years as circuit judge.

- At the age of 60, Samuel began appointing his sons as judges in Israel.

Scripture Search: Exercise 9

Find the Following Scriptures:

1. "Then the children of Israel did put away Baalim and Ashtaroth, and served the LORD only." **1 Samuel 7:**_____

2. "And fasted on that day, and said there, We have sinned against the LORD. And Samuel judged the children of Israel in Mizpeh." **1 Samuel 7:**_____

3. "And the LORD said unto Samuel, Hearken unto the voice of the people in all that they say unto thee: for they have not rejected thee, but they have rejected me, that I should not reign over them." **1 Samuel 8:**_____

4. "And Samuel heard all the words of the people, and he rehearsed them in the ears of the LORD." **1 Samuel 8:**_____

5. "If we go what shall we bring the man?" "And there is not a present to bring to the man of God: what have we?" **1 Samuel 9:**_____

6. "Is the seer here?" **1 Samuel 9:**_____

7. "And on whom is all the desire of Israel?" "Is not on thee, and on all thy father house?" **1 Samuel 9:**_____

8. "Am no I a Benjamite, of the smallest of the tribes of Israel?" "And my family the least of all the families?" Wherefore then speakest thou so to me?"
    1 Samuel 9:_____

Fill in the Blank: Exercise 10

1. And the children of Israel said to Samuel, Cease not to cry unto the LORD our God for us, that he will save us out of the _____ of the Philistines.

2. And his return was to Ramah; for there was his house; and there he _____ Israel; and there he built an altar unto the LORD.

3. And he will appoint him captains over _____, and captains over fifties; and will set them to ear his ground, and to reap his harvest, and to make his instruments of war, and _____ of his chariots.

4. And the servant answered Saul again, and said, Behold, I have here at hand the fourth part of a _____ of _____: that will I give to the man of God, to tell us our way.

Circle the Correct Word: Exercise 11

1. And it came to pass, while the ark abode in Kirjath-jearim, that the time was _____; for it was twenty years: and all the house of Israel lamented after the LORD.

LONG   **OVERDUE**

2. Then all the _____ of Israel gathered themselves together, and came to Samuel unto Ramah,

ELDERS   **SAINTS**

3. Now the LORD had told Samuel in his _____ a day before Saul came, saying,

EAR   **HAND**

True or False: Exercise 12

1. And he will take the tenth of your seed, and of your vineyards, and give to his officers, and to his servants.

TRUE OR FALSE

2. And the servant answered Saul again, and said, Behold, I have here at hand the fourth part of a shekel of silver: that will I give to the child of God, to tell us our way.

TRUE OR FALSE

READING ASSIGNMENT

1. Samuel as leader of all Israel. (1 Samuel 7:3-8)

2. Samuel; the last judge. (1 Samuel 7:15-17)

3. Samuel's influence fades. (1 Samuel 8:122)

4. Samuel's sons pervert justice. (1 Samuel 8:13)

5. Israel asks for a king. (1 Samuel 8:4-9)

6. Ways of a king described (1 Samuel 8:10-18)

7. Israel remains resolute. (1 Samuel 8:19-22)

8. God selects Israel's king. (1 Samuel 9:1-10)

REFLECTIONS

ISRAEL HAS HER KING!

Chapter 10

We left Samuel and Saul walking together, and Saul expecting to hear from Samuel the word of God. Now, here we have the anointing of Saul, the signs Samuel gave him and instructions; the accomplishment of those signs to the satisfaction of Saul; his return to his father's house; his public election by lot and solemn inauguration; and his return to his own city. (*Matthew Henry's Commentary on the Whole Bible, p. 399*)

Chapter 11

In this chapter, we have the first-fruits of Saul's government in the glorious rescue of Jabesh-Gilead out of the hands of the Ammonites. Let not Israel thence infer that therefore they did well to ask a king (God could and would have saved them without one); but let them admire God's goodness, that he did not reject them when they rejected him, and acknowledge his wisdom in the choice of the person whom, if he did not find fit, yet he made fit, for the great trust he called him to, and enabled, in some measure, to merit the crown by his public services, before it was fixed on his head by the public approbation. Here is the great extremity to which the city of Jabesh-Gilead, on the other side of Jordan, was reduced by the Ammonites; Saul's great readiness to come to their relief; the good success of his attempt; Saul's tenderness towards those who had opposed him; and the public confirmation and recognition of his election to the government. (*Matthew Henry's Commentary on the Whole Bible, p. 401*)

Chapter 12

We left the general assembly of the states together in the close of the foregoing chapter. In this chapter, we have Samuel's speech to them when he resigned the government into the hands of Saul in which he clears himself from all suspicion or imputation of mismanagement, while the administration was in his hands. He reminds them of the great things God had done for them and for their fathers. He sets before them good and evil, the blessing and the curse. He awakens them to regard what he said to them by calling to God for thunder. He encourages them with hopes that all should be well. This is his farewell sermon to that august assembly and Saul's coronation sermon. (*Matthew Henry's Commentary on the Whole Bible, p. 402*)

SAUL's PROCESS OF LOSING HIS SPIRITUAL INHERITANCE (KINGDOM)

I. STUBBORNNESS

- Having not understanding after instruction. (Psalms. 32:9)

- Disloyal or unfaithful to God. (Psalms 78:8)

- Stiff-necked and iron-forehead (Isaiah 48:4; Exodus 32:9: Ezekiel 3:9)

- Refuses to listen and refuses to give honor. (Malachi 2:2)

- Refuses to heed the call. (Isaiah 65:12; Jeremiah 7:13; Romans 10:21)

- Does not trust in the Lord. (2 Kings 17:14-15)

- Refuses to listen to the prophets, preachers or messengers of God. (Luke 16:31)

II. <u>SELF-WILLED</u>

- Refusing to take heed to the commandments of God. (Deuteronomy1:43)

- Failure to rest in quietness and confidence in the Lord. (Isaiah 30:15)

- Not afraid to speak evil or despise authority. (2 Peters 2:10)

- Hard-hearted. (Psalms 95:8; Proverbs 28:14)

- *Often* reproved or rebuked. (Proverbs 29:1; Isaiah 42:25)

- Having an impenitent heart (having or showing no regret or sorrow for sin or misbehavior). (Romans 2:5)

- Deceitfulness of sin. (Hebrew 2:13)

III. <u>SELF-DECEPTION</u>

- High self-esteem (flattering themselves too much to detect or hate sin. (Psalms 36:2)

- Conceit. (Galatians 6:3)

- Careless hearing. (James 1:22)

- An unbridled tongue. (James 1:26)

- Sanctimony (holier-than-thou; making an exaggerated show of holiness or moral superiority). (1 John 1:8)

- False trust (trusting in wealth and destroying others). (Psalms 52:7)

- Spiritual bondage (heart is deluded and misleading). (Isaiah 44:20)

IV. <u>SELF-EXALTATION</u>

- One who puts himself before others. (Proverbs 25:6-7)

- One who seeks his own glory. (Proverbs 25:27)

- One who loves transgression and strife. (Proverbs 17:19)

- One who exalts himself. (Isaiah 14:13-14; Obadiah 4; Matthew 23:12)

- One who boasts of himself. (Psalms 10:3; Proverbs 25:14; Psalms 49:6; James 4:16)

- Conceited (one who is wise in his own eyes). (Proverbs 3:7; Proverbs 26:12; Isaiah 5:21)

- Prideful. (Psalms 10:2; Proverbs 16:18; Proverbs 21:4)

Obedience is more important than all forms of religion—sacrifices, offerings, rituals, ceremonies. It is the chief end of all true religion. Rebellion and stubbornness are a manifestation of failure in conforming to truth. Obedience requires this response:

- Wholeheartedness (unstinted devotion). (Deuteronomy 26:16)

- God's word in your heart and out of your mouth. (Joshua1:8)

- Walking in the ways of God. (Jeremiah 7:23)

- Doing God's will and practicing God's Word. (Matthew 7:21; Luke 8:21)

- Obeying God rather than men. (Acts 5:29)

- Completing the tasks assigned by God. (Joshua 11:15)

- Learning from trials, tribulations and tests. (Hebrew 5:8)

Scripture Search: Exercise 13

Find the Following Scriptures:

1. "Is it not because the Lord hath anointed thee to be captain over his inheritance?" **1 Samuel 10:**_____

2. "What shall I do for my son" **1 Samuel 10:**_____

3. "What is this that is come unto the son of Kish? Is Saul also among the prophets? **1 Samuel 10:**_____

4. "And one of the same places answered and said, but who is their father? There fore it became a proverb is Saul also among prophets?"
    1 Samuel 10:_____

5. "Saul's uncle said unto him and to his servant, whither went ye?"
    1 Samuel 10:_____

6. "What shall I do for my son" **1 Samuel 10:**_____

7. "What aileth the people that they weep" **1 Samuel 11:**_____

8. "And Saul said, 'There shall not a man be put to death this day: for to day the LORD hath wrought salvation in Israel.'"
    1 Samuel 11:_____

9. "Whose ox have I taken? Or whose ass have I taken? Or whom have I defrauded? Whom have I oppressed? Or of whose hand have received any bribe to blind mine eyes therewith?"
    1 Samuel 12:_____

10. "Is it not wheat harvest today?" **1 Samuel 12:**_____

Fill in the Blank: Exercise 14

1. And it was so, that when he had turned his back to go from Samuel, God gave him another _____: and all those signs came to pass that day.

2. And Saul said, There shall not a man be put to death this day: for to day the LORD hath wrought _____ in Israel.

3. And they said, Thou hast not defrauded us, nor _____ us, neither hast thou taken ought of any man's hand.

4. So Samuel called unto the LORD; and the LORD sent thunder and rain that day: and all the people _____ feared the LORD and Samuel.

Circle the Correct Word: Exercise 15

1. And the Spirit of the LORD will come upon thee, and thou shalt _____ with them, and shalt be turned into another man.

PROPHESY   **WHISPER**

2. And the Spirit of God came upon Saul when he heard those tidings, and his _____ was kindled greatly.

ANGER   **HAPPINESS**

3. So Samuel called unto the LORD; and the LORD sent _____ and rain that day: and all the people greatly feared the LORD and Samuel.

THUNDER   **CLOUDS**

True or False: Exercise 16

1. And when he had made an end of prophesying, he came to the high place.

TRUE OR FALSE

2. For the LORD will not forsake his people for his great name's sake: because it hath pleased the LORD to make you his enemy.

TRUE OR FALSE

READING ASSIGNMENTS

1. Samuel poured oil on Saul. (1 Samuel 10:1)

2. Saul prophesied. (1 Samuel 10:10)

3. Samuel introduces Saul as King. (1 Samuel 10:23-24)

4. Saul wins public support. (1 Samuel 11:1-15)

5. Samuel's farewell speech. (1 Samuel 12:1-3)

6. Samuel called down thunder and rain. (1 Samuel 12:17-18)

7. Samuel's warning to Israel. (1 Samuel 12:23-25)

REFLECTIONS

SAUL IS REBELLIOUS
AND DISHONEST

Chapter 13

In this chapter, we discover that while Samuel was joined in commission with Saul things went well, But now that Saul began to reign alone, all went to decay, and Samuel's words began to be fulfilled: "You shall be consumed, both you and your king;" for never was the state of Israel further gone in a consumption than in this chapter. Saul appears here a very silly prince, infatuated in his counsels, invaded by his neighbors, deserted by his soldiers, disordered in his own spirit, and sacrificing in confusion, and rejected of God from being king. (*Matthew Henry's Commentary on the Whole Bible, p. 404*)

Chapter 14

We left the host of Israel in a very ill posture in the close of the foregoing chapter. We saw in them no wisdom, nor strength, nor goodness to give us ground to expect anything other than that they should all be cut off by the army of the Philistines. Yet here we find that infinite power which works without means, and that infinite goodness which gives without merit, glorified in a happy turn to their affairs, that still Samuel's words may be made good: "The Lord will not forsake his people, for his great name's sake. In this chapter we have, the host of the Philistines trampled upon and triumphed over by the faith and courage of Jonathan, who unknown to his father with his armor-bearer only made a brave attack upon them, encouraging himself in the Lord his God. He challenged them, and upon their acceptance of the challenge, charged them with such fury, or rather such faith, that he put them to flight, and set them one against another, which gave opportunity to Saul and his forces to follow the blow and gain a victory. In the close we have a general account of Saul's exploits and of his family. (*Matthew Henry's Commentary on the Whole Bible, p. 405*)

Chapter 15

In this chapter, we have the final rejection of Saul from being king, for his disobedience to God's command in not utterly destroying the Amalekites. By his wars and victories, he hoped to magnify and perpetuate his own name and honor, but by his mismanagement of them, he ruined himself and laid his honor in the dust. Here is the commission God gave him to destroy the Amalekites, with a command to do it utterly, Saul's preparation for this expedition, his success, and partial execution of this commission, his examination before Samuel and sentence passed upon him, notwithstanding the many frivolous pleas he made to excuse himself, the slaying of Agag, and Samuel's final farewell to Saul. (*Matthew Henry's Commentary on the Whole Bible, p. 408*)

I. MILITARY DOMINANCE (1 Samuel 13:19)

Samuel's leadership kept the Philistines from occupying Israel (1 Samuel 7:13). However, no one could question the Philistines' military dominance. They had outposts in several central Israelite towns (1 Samuel 10:5; 13:3) and most importantly, they kept a monopoly on iron weapons by outlawing local blacksmiths. Only the royal family of Israel possessed a sword or a spear (1 Samuel 13:22), presumably weapons that had been smuggled in and hidden.

Bethhaven—house of vanity where Saul made a foolish oath, of which Jonathan violated and the people suffered.

II. REBELLION DEFINED

Rebellion—a revolt, uprising, insurgence, mutiny, rising; the opposition or defiance of authority, accepted moral codes or social conventions; an organized attempt to overthrow a government or other authority by the use of violence.

"Rebellion" in Hebrew . . .

1) **Carah (saw raw)**, meaning apostasy, defection, turning aside, withdrawal: a) defection of moral or legal offenses; b) renunciation of religious or political belief or allegiance; c) withdrawal, the act or condition of taking something away or no longer taking part in something.

2) **Pesha (peh shah)**, meaning, transgression or rebellion: a) transgression against individuals; b) transgression nation against nation; c) transgression against God.

III. THE EIGHT GREAT EVILS OF SAUL'S FOOLISH CURSE

- Caused the innocent to suffer. (1 Samuel 14:24-30, 37-46)
- Helped to defeat his own cause. (1 Samuel 14:30)
- Caused the people to be so faint that they committed sin in eating the flesh of animals improperly killed. (1 Samuel 14:32-34)
- Caused God to refuse to answer him that day. (1 Samuel 14:37)
- Caused all Israel to refuse to answer their king. (1 Samuel 14:39)
- Caused all Israel to defy their king. (1 Samuel 14:45)
- Caused a great victory to be cut short, making it necessary to fight the Philistines later. (1 Samuel 14:46-42; 17:1-58)
- No doubt caused his own death. Had he destroyed the Philistines when he had the opportunity, they perhaps would not have fought him at the time he died. (1 Samuel 28:1-31; 13)

IV. SAUL'S VICTORIES

- Moab (1 Samuel 14:47)
- Ammon (1 Samuel 14:47; 11:1-15)
- Edom (1 Samuel 14:47)
- Zobah (a kingdom between Damascus and Euphrates
- Philistia (1 Samuel 14 1-47, 52; 17:1-55
- Amalek (1 Samuel 14:47; 14:1-35)

V. SAUL's OFFSPRING

- **Jonathan** (Jehovah has given), the eldest. (1 Samuel 13:2)
- **Ishui** (equality), called Ishbosheth (man of shame) (1 Samuel14:49), made kind after Saul (2 Samuel 2:8-15; 3:7-15); also called Eshbaal. (1 Chronicles 3:33; 9:39)
- **Melchishua** (king of help) (1 Samuel 14:49; 31:1); also called Malchishua
- (1 Chronicles 8:33; 9:39; 10:2)
- **Abinadab** (father of liberality) (1 Samuel 31:2; 1 Chronicles 8:33; 9:39; 10:2)
- **Ahinoam** (brother of grace), wife of Saul (1 Samuel 14:50). David also had a wife by this name (1 Samuel 25:43; 27:3 30:5; 2 Samuel 2:2)
- **Merab** (increase) and **Michal** (brook) Saul's two daughters (1 Samuel 14:49; 18:17-28)
- **Ahimaaz** (brother of anger), there were 3 with this name, Saul's father-in-law (14:50); the son of Zadok, the priest (2 Samuel 15:27, 36; 17:17, 20); officer of Solomon (1 Kings 4:15)
- **Abner** (father of light), Saul's uncle and military leader. (1 Samuel 14:50-51; 10:14-16)
- **Ner** (light), father of Abner. (1 Samuel 14:50-51)
- **Kish** (bow), there were five different men named Kish; the most prominent was the father of Saul. (1 Chronicles 24:29)
- **Abiel** (father of strength) (1 Samuel 14:51; 9:1)
- **Abialbon** (2 Samuel 23:31). This was the fulfillment of the word of Samuel (1 Samuel 8:16-18.)

VI. SAUL'S THREE-FOLD COMMISSION (1 Samuel 15:3)

Saul's three-fold commission fulfilled God's purpose, which was prophesied approximately 500 years before it's fulfillment. (Exodus 17:14-16)

COMMISSION #1 Go and smite Amalek.

COMMISSION #2 Utterly destroy all that they own.

COMMISSION #3 Spare them not, but slay men, women, infants, suckling children, oxen, sheep, camels, and asses.

THE AMALEKITES

An ancient wandering tribe descended from Esau's grandson, Amalek (Genesis 36:12, 16; 1 Chronicles 1:36). The main territory of the Amalekites was in the Sinai Peninsula and in the Negev, the southern part of present day Israel. However, they roamed widely throughout the territory, later settled by the people of Israel. Throughout the Old Testament, the Amalekites were bitter foes of the Israelites.

The Amalekites are first mentioned in the time of Abraham, when a group of kings under the leadership of Chedorlaomer defeated Amalek. (Genesis 14:7) At the time of Israel's journey through the wilderness, the Amalekites lived in the southern part of the land promised to Israel. The Amalekites attacked the Israelites, but Joshua later defeated them in the battle at Rephidim. (Exodus 17:8-16) Because of their treacherous attacks, Moses declared that God would continually wage war against them. (Exodus 17:14-16)

- A people inhabiting the country south of Idumea and east of the Red Sea.
- (Numbers 13:29; 14:25; 1 Samuel 15:7; 27:8)
- Defeated by Chedorlaomer. (Genesis 14:7)
- Defeated by Joshua. (Exodus 17:8,13)
- Defeated by Gideon. (Judges 7)

- Defeated by Saul. (1 Samuel 14:47,48; 15:1-33)
- Defeated by David. (1 Samuel 27:8,9; 30:1-20)
- Defeated by the Simeonites. (1 Chronicles 4:42,43)
- Defeated the Israelites. (Numbers 14:45; Judges 3:13)
- Israel was commanded to destroy the Amalekites. (Deuteronomy 25:17-19; 1 Samuel 28:18)
- Prophecies against the Amalekites. (Exodus 17:14,16; Numbers 24:20)

THE KENITES

The name of a wandering tribe of people who were associated with the Midianites (Judges 1:16) and later with the Amalekites (1 Samuel 15:6). The Kenites lived in the desert regions of Sinai, Midian, Edom, Amalek and the Negev. The Bible first mentions the Kenites as one of the groups that lived in Canaan during the time of Abraham (Genesis 15:19). Their territory was to be taken by the Israelites (Numbers 24:21-22). The Kenites were metal craftsmen who may have traced their ancestry to TUBAL-CAIN (Gen 4:22). Around the time of Israel's exodus from Egypt, the Kenites showed kindness to Israel (1 Samuel 15:6). Moses' father-in-law, Jethro, is called a Midianite (Exodus 18:1) and a Kenite (Judges 1:16). Some scholars suggest the skill in smelting and casting the golden calf (Exodus 32) and the bronze serpent (Numbers 21) may have been learned by Moses from the Kenites.

VII. THE SAULISH SPIRIT—Religious and Prideful

Summary of the Saulish Spirit

- Self-centered and arrogant.
- The religious spirit clouds the Holy Spirit's convictions and dilutes God's Word, giving you a false assurance of your relationship with God.
- Pride always justifies your feelings and actions. It elevates self above everything and everyone.

- Saul turned against Samuel because of his unwillingness to submit to God and to godly leadership.

The Saulish Spirit . . .

- Works on God's chosen people and their family members.
- Causes you to turn on those who try to help you.
- Jealous of other's accomplishments.
- Unconsciously disobeys God.
- Retaliates against leadership in the face of correction.
- Operates in areas to which you have not been assigned (Ex. Saul tried to do the priestly duties).
- Tries to harm God's people and God's anointed.
- Lacks humility.
- The belief that you are always right.
- More concerned about reputation and acceptance.
- Fears people and not God.

Scriptures describing the Saulish Spirit

- Saul failed as leader. He feared the people. (1 Samuel 15:23-24)
- Jealousy consumed Saul's heart. (1 Samuel 18:8-9)
- Saul threw the javelin at David in an attempt to kill him. (1 Samuel 20:33)
- Saul killed priests because refused to disclose David's whereabouts. (1 Samuel 22:19)
- Saul was possessed by an evil spirit of religion. (1 Samuel 16:14, 18:10)
- Saul lashed out at the prophet. (1 Samuel 15:27-28)
- Saul played priest for a day. (1 Samuel 13:9-12)
- Saul sought help from a witch. (1 Samuel 28:1-9)
- Saul committed suicide. (1 Samuel 31:4-6)

VIII. THE SAULISH SPIRIT QUIZ

- Do I get jealous of other believers or ministries?
- Do I lash out at my leaders when I am corrected?
- Do I always have to be confronted with my sin because I don't see it in time?
- Do I make excuses for my sinful words and actions?
- Do I that feel I can survive life without spiritual leadership?
- Do I sometimes despise God's people when they are anointed to worship and praise before God?
- Do I often think more highly of myself than I should think?

Scripture Search: Exercise 17

Find the Following Scriptures:

1. "What hast thou done?" **1 Samuel 13:**_____

2. "But all the Israelites went down to the Philistines, to sharpen every man his share, and his coulter, and his axe, and his mattock." **1 Samuel 13:**_____

3. "How much more if haply the people had eaten, freely to day of the spoil of their enemies which they found? For had there not been now a much greater slaughter among the Philistines?" **1 Samuel 14:**_____

4. "Shall I go down after the Philistines? Wilt thou deliver them into the hand of Israel?" **1 Samuel 14:**_____

5. "And the people said unto Saul shall Jonathan die, who hath wrought this great salvation in Israel?" **1 Samuel 14:**_____

6. "What meanest then this bleating of the sheep in mine ears an the lowing o f the oxen which I hear?" **1 Samuel 15:**_____

7. "When thou wast little in thine own sight wast thou not made the head of the tribes of Israel and the Lord anointed thee king over Israel?" **1 Samuel 15:**_____

8. "Wherefore then dist thou not obey the voice of the Lord but dist fly upon the spoil and dist evil in the sight of the Lord?" **1 Samuel 15:**_____

9. "Hath the Lord as great delight in burnt offerings and sacrifices as obeying the voice of the Lord." **1 Samuel 15:**_____

Fill in the Blank: Exercise 18

1. And Samuel said to Saul, Thou hast done foolishly: thou hast not kept the commandment of the LORD thy God, which he commanded thee: for now would the LORD have established thy _____ upon Israel for ever.

2. And Jonathan said to the young man that bare his armor, Come, and let us go over unto the garrison of these uncircumcised: it may be that the _____ will work for us: for there is no restraint to the _____ to save by many or by few.

3. So the LORD saved _____ that day: and the battle passed over unto Bethhaven.

4. And Saul gathered the people together, and _____ them in Telaim, two hundred thousand footmen, and ten thousand men of Judah.

Circle the Correct Word: Exercise 19

1. Saul reigned _____; and when he had reigned two years over Israel,

SEVEN YEARS   **ONE YEAR**

2. And Saul built an _____ unto the LORD: the same was the first altar that he built unto the LORD.

BARN   **ALTAR**   **HOUSE**

3. Then Samuel said unto Saul, Stay, and I will tell thee what the _____ hath said to me this night. And he said unto him, Say on.

LORD   **BISHOP**   **FIRST LADY**

True or False: Exercise 20

1. And Saul gathered the people together, and numbered them in Telaim, two hundred thousand footmen, and ten thousand men of Africa.

TRUE OR FALSE

2. Wherefore then didst thou not obey the voice of the LORD, but didst fly upon the spoil, and didst evil in the sight of the LORD?

TRUE OR FALSE

READING ASSIGNMENT

1. Saul prepares for war. (1 Samuel 13:1-5)

2. Samuel rebukes Saul. (1 Samuel 13:11-13)

3. Israel without weapons. (1 Samuel 13:22)

4. Jonathan had faith in God. (1 Samuel 14:6)

5. Israel army sinned against God. (1 Samuel 14:33)

6. Saul's reign summarized. (1 Samuel 14:47-52)

7. Samuel gives Saul instructions concerning the Amalekites. (1 Samuel 15:1-6)

8. Saul rejected as king. (1 Samuel 15:16-17)

9. Saul violates the ban. (1 Samuel 15:19)

10. Samuel leaves Saul. (1 Samuel 15:247-33)

REFLECTIONS

ANSWER KEY

Chapters 1, 2, 3

1. 1 Samuel 1:8
2. 1 Samuel 1:14
3. 1 Samuel 1:23
4. 1 Samuel 1:25
5. 1 Samuel 2:27
6. 1Samuel 2:28
7. 1 Samuel 2:29
8. 1 Samuel 3:11
9. 1 Samuel 3:17
10. 1 Samuel 3:21

FILL IN THE BLANK

1. HANNAH
2. COMPLAINT—GRIEF
3. HABITATION—ISRAEL
4. BEERSHEBA

CIRCLE THE CORRECT WORD

1. DRUNK
2. SACRIFICE
3. CALLLED—ANSWERED

TRUE OR FALSE

1. FALSE
2. TRUE

Chapters 4, 5, 6

1. 1 Samuel 4:3
2. 1 Samuel 4:6
3. 1 Samuel 4:8
4. 1 Samuel 4:14
5. 1 Samuel 4:16
6. 1 Samuel 5:8
7. 1 Samuel 6:2
8. 1 Samuel 6:4
9. 1 Samuel 6:6
10. 1 Samuel 6:20

FILL IN THE BLANK

1. HEBREWS
2. DEPARTED—HUSBAND
3. DESTROYED
4. MICE

THE CORRECT WORD

1. PHILISTINES
2. ASHDOD
3. CALVES

TRUE OR FALSE

1. TRUE

2. TRUE

Chapters 7, 8, 9

1. 1 Samuel 7:4
2. 1 Samuel 7:6
3. 1 Samuel 8:7
4. 1 Samuel 8:21
5. 1 Samuel 9:7
6. 1 Samuel 9:11
7. 1 Samuel 9:20
8. 1 Samuel 9:21

FILL IN THE BLANK

1. HAND
2. JUDGED
3. THOUSANDS—INSTRUMENTS
4. SHEKEL—SILVER

CIRCLE THE CORRECT WORD

1. LONG
2. ELDERS
3. EAR

TRUE OR FALSE

1. TRUE
2. FALSE

Chapters 10, 11, 12

1. 1 Samuel 10:1
2. 1 Samuel 10:2
3. 1 Samuel 10:11-12, 14
4. 1 Samuel 10:24
5. 1 Samuel 1 Sam 11:5
6. 1 Samuel 11:13
7. 1 Samuel 12:3
8. 1 Samuel 12:17

FILL IN THE BLANK:

1. HEART
2. SALVATION
3. OPPRESSED
4. GREATLY

CIRCLE THE CORRECT WORD

1. PROPHESY
2. ANGER
3. THUNDER

TRUE OR FALSE

1. TRUE
2. FALSE

Chapters 13, 14, 15

1. 1 Samuel 13:11
2. 1 Samuel 13:20
3. 1 Samuel 14:30

4. 1 Samuel 14:37
5. 1 Samuel 14:45
6. 1 Samuel 15:14
7. 1 Samuel 1 Sam 15:17
8. 1 Samuel 15:19
9. 1 Samuel 15:22

FILL IN THE BLANK:

1. KINGDOM
2. LORD—LORD
3. ISRAEL—NUMBERED

CIRCLE THE CORRECT WORD

1. SEVEN YEARS
2. ALTAR
3. LORD

TRUE OR FALSE

1. FALSE
2. TRUE